Who is living next Door?
The Life Of Riley

written by Deborah Tant

Books by Deborah Tant

Series - The Life of Riley
Book 1 - Things that bite in the Night
Book 2 - Around our Swimming Pool
Book 3 - Who is Living Next Door?

––––––––––––

Snowball - The Humpback Whale

Riley

DEDICATION

A special thank you to my husband Tony for his support and patience. To my beautiful nieces Sarah, Jessica and Anna and their gorgeous children for their on-going support.

Text Copyright © 2023 by Deborah Tant Illustration
Copyright © 2023 by Deborah Tant

The moral rights of the author have been asserted.

All rights reserved
No part of this book may be reproduced in any form by any electronic or mechanical means, including information storage and retrieval systems, without written permission from the author, except for the use of brief quotations in a book review.

Publisher: Deborah Tant - Powered by Above
Author: Deborah Tant
Illustrator: Claudia Hoffmann-Kaeufer

2nd Edition
Paperback ISBN: 978-0-6459450-2-7
E-book ISBN: 978-06459450-0-3
Hardback ISBN: 978-0-6459450-1-0

A catalog record or this book is available from the National Library of Australia

www.poweredbyabove.com
poweredbyabove@poweredbyabove.com

Riley and Jazz went for a walk, past the farm where the cows can talk.
Past the horses that are their friends, to a field that is usually empty, with not even hens.

Here they saw five large camels having a sleep.

Jazz said *"What on earth are they?*

They don't look like sheep!".

Riley said *"They are camels, can't you see?"*

Jazz said *"No, I don't, can you explain that to me?"*

Riley said *"With Camels we can climb aboard and fly away and see the world from the Milky Way"*.

Jazz replied *"Fly away to where? How does that work?"*
Riley explained *"You make a wish, think of beautiful things.*
Smile with your heart and let it grow wings.
Before you know it, you will be flying to the Milky Way through the sky,
with rainbow colored elephants passing you by".

"WOW! I want to do that" said Jazz to Riley.

"Shall we go and ask them ever so nicely"?

"Hello Mrs. Camel we are Riley and Jazz".

"You can call me Elsa from Razzamatazz.

What can I do for you two boys"? She asked in a very sweet voice and with a beautiful poise.

Riley and Jazz replied
"We would like very much to climb up high,
of you and your friends and go into the sky.
To make a wish and think of beautiful things.
To smile with our heart and let it grow wings.
Then we can fly to the Milky Way through
the sky,
with rainbow colored elephants passing us by.

"Humm" Elsa from Razzamatazz said.

"To the Milky Way and back again.

I will need to check with my friend.

It won't be today as they are aching.

Come back tomorrow when dawn is breaking".

Off home they ran, imaginations going crazy.

They wanted to tell the world but it all sounded so hazy.

Down the hill and up again,

to tell the cows and their horses that were eating grain.

Monty-Moo is at home, he won't believe what we have done.

Tomorrow first thing is going to be so much fun.

The camels next door and their magical wings,

it is going to take place tomorrow first thing.

"Monty-Moo you won't believe what we have seen.

The most magical thing that has ever been.

Camels everywhere,

they are taking us on a ride we can all share.

To make a wish and think of beautiful things.

To smile with our heart and let it grow wings.

Then we can fly to the Milky Way through the sky,

with rainbow colored elephants passing us by".

That night after their bath and when it was time for bed,
Mama was tucking them in and kissing their head.
They closed their eyes and saw Elsa from Razzamatazz,
she had two of her friends and asked *"Are you ready Jazz?"*

Jazz said *"Come on boys it's time to go!"*,

so off they went with a camel called Beau.

Over the fields and mountains so high,

into the clouds where they saw Angels fly.

When they got to their destination, the Milky Way,

they saw rainbow colored elephants and camels rolling in hay.

Riley said to Jazz "There are no bounds to what heaven can be,

it's up to you in what you want to see."

Before they knew it Elsa was telling them it was time to go,

and asked "Are you ready Beau?"

She said "Boys, make a wish, think of beautiful things.

Smile with your heart and let it grow wings.

Then we can fly to the Milky Way through the sky,

with rainbow colored elephants passing us by".

This is where beautiful dreams are made,
with happy hearts and happy days.
Where children's smiles are big in size,
where boys and girls sleep sweetly until sunrise.

Sweet dreams everybody.
Good Night.

Elsa from Razzamatazz

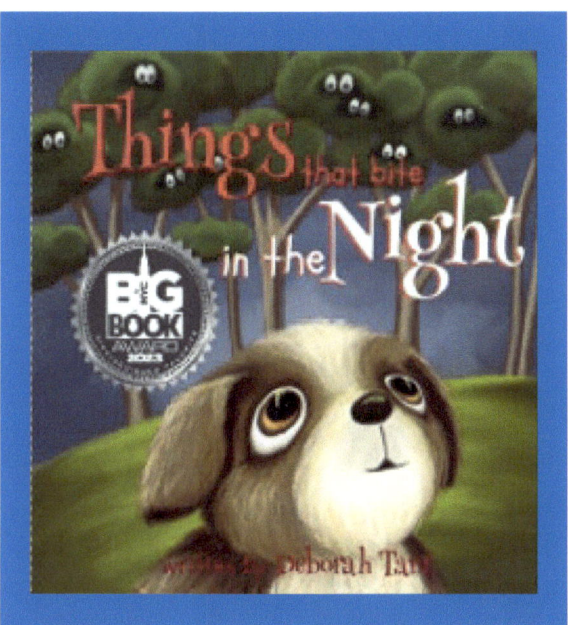

written by Deborah Tant

www.ingramcontent.com/pod-product-compliance
Lightning Source LLC
Chambersburg PA
CBHW041428010526
44107CB00045B/1534